Grief Land

Mary Burritt
    Christiansen
Poetry Series

Mary Burritt Christiansen Poetry Series
Hilda Raz, Series Editor

The Mary Burritt Christiansen Poetry Series publishes two to four books a year that engage and give voice to the realities of living, working, and experiencing the West and the Border as places and as metaphors. The purpose of the series is to expand access to, and the audience for, quality poetry, both single volumes and anthologies, that can be used for general reading as well as in classrooms.

Also available in the Mary Burritt Christiansen Poetry Series:

Feel Puma: Poems by Ray Gonzalez
The Shadowgraph: Poems by James Cihlar
Crosscut: Poems by Sean Prentiss
The Music of Her Rivers: Poems by Renny Golden
to cleave: poems by Barbara Rockman
After Party: Poems by Noah Blaustein
The News as Usual: Poems by Jon Kelly Yenser
Gather the Night: Poems by Katherine DiBella Seluja
The Handyman's Guide to End Times: Poems by Juan J. Morales
Rain Scald: Poems by Tacey M. Atsitty

For additional titles in the Mary Burritt Christiansen Poetry Series, please visit unmpress.com.

Grief
Land

POEMS

CARRIE SHIPERS

UNIVERSITY OF NEW MEXICO PRESS ⌒ ALBUQUERQUE

ISBN 978-0-8263-6167-7 (paper)
ISBN 978-0-8263-6168-4 (electronic)

Library of Congress Control Number: 2020935706

Cover photograph by Gabriele Diwald on Unsplash
Designed by Felicia Cedillos
Composed in Adobe Caslon Pro 10/14

FOR RANDAL

Contents

SECTION THREE

SECTION ONE

GRIEF LAND

On the road to Grief Land, you pass other attractions you'd prefer—
zoo, water park, dirt track for monster trucks, haunted asylum

on a hill—but it's too late to change your plans. Admission
costs more than you'd thought. Your coupon is expired and no

discounts apply. Inside the gates, the landscape you remember
has been changed. Where you expect a carousel, a band shell

stocked with elderly trombones. In place of a photo booth,
a funhouse full of foggy mirrors. At least the rides are still

the same: rollercoaster, Ferris wheel, cages that rotate upside down.
You start with the one that you like least—barrel that spins,

pins you to the wall while the bottom drops away. Despite rust
and peeling paint, accidents are rare and so far never fatal.

You're safe if you stay seated, keep hands and feet inside the car,
obey the teenage operators who make sure your lap bar's locked,

wish you an awesome ride. At Grief Land, you crave cotton candy,
funnel cake, corn dogs striped with mustard you drip on your shirt.

Your stomach hurts even before the kettle corn, nachos, cherry
snow cone leaking in the dirt. No matter what the forecast says,

damp air forms a sticky film. Umbrellas aren't allowed,
so during daily showers people shelter in the gift shop

and arcade. Being near so many bodies crowds your breath,
but far-off lightning means you're trapped until clouds clear.

You don't doubt you deserve a prize from game booths rigged
to let you win, or that once your arms are tired, the giant

blow-up hammer, stuffed dog with mournful eyes, won't seem
worth keeping. The longer your day at Grief Land lasts,

the more unease you feel among the smeary clowns, groundskeepers
trailing smoke as they sweep up debris. Your feet and knees

are sore, but even when you find a place to sit you can't keep still—
you need one more thing to make your trip complete,

and only walking will remind you what it is. Rising darkness
amplifies music from the rides, songs you heard once

at a high school dance or college party, this morning in the car.
You watch packs of people rushing toward their fun, their smiles

forced and laughter frantic, and decide you're not like them at all.
When you're ready to leave, it's hard to find your way. Twice

you try to follow exit signs and wind up deeper in the park.
You consider climbing the fence fronting the road, then see

its row of barbs. Frustration makes your headache worse,
as does the whine and blare of the PA, parties anxious to meet

at the grandstand or fountain. After a long search for your car,
which is much farther from the gates than you remember,

you drive home bleary-eyed and hunched over the wheel.
Your visit wasn't quite what you'd been hoping, but you know

it's pointless to complain, swear you won't go back. Grief Land
may not be your favorite place, but no one stays away for good.

One morning just after I arrived,
a man walked past my building
singing Springsteen, then yelled *Fuck*
over and over. By the time I got up
to look, he'd disappeared, or at least
gone silent. Everywhere I walk my dog
we find chicken bones and coins—
mostly pennies, but sometimes dimes
and quarters. Also playing cards,
which raises questions—why people
have so many decks, why they wear out
so fast. I don't like donuts very much,
but I can always find a Dunkin'
when I need to turn around.
Because I'm still afraid to drive
downtown, I get my hair cut
and teeth cleaned in a suburb that starts
a few streets over. At first I resisted
the Rhode Island left, but I've come
to appreciate how practical it is.

I love how people pronounce *car*,
coffee and my first name. They seem
to say whatever's on their minds,
often loudly and in public places.
At the DMV: *I be promotin' my shit*.
The library: *I take the bus because
I don't have time*. The bank: *My son's
a friggin' leech*. At the park, grown men
play baseball in full uniform in front
of signs that say *Police Take Notice*,
which is either a threat or a request.
Hundreds of bottle caps—mostly
Corona Light—shine in dirt that's more
like sand. In summer, the forecast

on the local news includes tides,
wave heights and safe sun time.

Even the grocery stores are different.
I can't buy alcohol or mail my packages.
Goya gets most of one entire aisle,
pasta and sauce another, so many kinds
I'll never try them all. Six weeks
after I moved, my father died.
He was never going to visit because
he didn't fly, but he said I should live
where I was happy. I don't always
remember that he's dead. I catch myself
eyeing lottery machines for tickets
I could send, practicing stories
about traffic. Sometimes I pretend
the coins I pick up are from him,
but I was finding change before he died.

Narrative Medicine

It bothered me when people at the hospital
misunderstood my husband's story. They asked
why he didn't treat the diabetes he'd never had,
heart condition he'd just learned about, how long

his kidney had been weak, why his leg wound—
only a few days old, inflicted by a wheelchair
steered too fast—wasn't completely healed.
I didn't speak for him unless he asked me to,

but when he was worn out with pain, same questions
every shift, I tried to outline facts and not frustrations.
Because I wasn't always there—because sometimes
he was scared and confused—I couldn't stop the staff

from hearing what they wanted to, like when
the discharge nurse asked *Who takes care of you
at home?* and thought his answer meant more
than just recently. By then he'd been admitted

three times in three weeks. He couldn't walk
without support, eat food he had to chew, manage
the toilet on his own. Even though I wanted him
in rehab rather than at home, I also wanted to explain:

In our regular life, he didn't need a caregiver.
Even worse was when family and friends I told
about his death insisted he'd expected it. Their evidence
was in the packages he'd sent: his mother's bible,

stepdad's knife, souvenirs from his fraternity, stacks
of labeled photographs, a piece of goalpost painted
Tiger gold. It seemed unkind to argue that in June,
we'd moved to our fourth state in fourteen years,

and we knew we weren't having kids to pass
our keepsakes to. Before we left Wisconsin,
I recycled all our wedding cards, gave my dress
to Goodwill. He spent hours sifting boxes untouched

in the five years since Nebraska. In Rhode Island,
his desk was a mess of maps, menus, plans
to shop for furniture, visit the Viking rock
he'd read about, take the train to Boston and New York.

When the doctors recommended high-risk surgery,
he was afraid but said he wasn't giving up,
would rather live with disability than not at all.
Then doctors changed their minds and he died anyway.

I understand why people who weren't there
want to believe that he'd accepted and prepared—
because it hurts them less than what I saw
unfold: In just over a month, his minor illness

became serious, then critical, then grave, then ended
in the worst possible way. I'm sure his doctors
have a version, too—that he was very sick
and should've been in their care sooner, that his outcome

was unavoidable though they did everything
they could. For all the questions my husband
was asked when he was ill, there are things
I'll never know: Whether he really thought—

before he got so sick or after—that he was going
to die. If he decided not to mention it or said it
in a way I failed to hear. If he thought his silence
was protecting me and if in fact it was. If there's one

true story of his death and whether it's the one I tell.

Death Is Not an Emergency

After Erin Belieu

At least, yours wasn't. For a week, I sat beside your bed
waiting for doctors to confirm what I already knew, or thought

I knew, or feared so much I practiced thinking it was true
in order to protect myself. The last time we talked, you sat up

and made sense, made jokes and told me to go home, order
pizza and relax. That was before I learned *la belle indifférence*,

how sometimes patients rally just before the worst,
how no one knows quite how or why. The next morning,

my phone rang just as I reached the hospital: Code Blue,
CPR, eight minutes before your heart restarted. That night,

I was afraid that if I left you'd die, afraid that if I stayed
you'd hang on for my sake. I changed your directive to

Do Not Resuscitate, sat trembling on a bench before
I drove away, woke up every hour trying to sense if you

were still alive. Therapeutic hypothermia: They wrapped you
in ice, lowered your core temperature to forestall damage

to your brain, then made you warm again. The first CT
showed no physical harm, was offset by the slowing of activity

the EEG revealed. And still they said you might wake up,
the slowing due to sedatives or cooling, other factors not

well understood. I walked laps of the parking lot, cried
into my phone, sat in the sunlit lobby feeling terrified.

I read beside your bed, then stood and touched your arm,
forehead, ankle, thumb, anywhere there wasn't something

in my way. I told you I needed you to come back soon,
told you the love and prayers our friends were sending.

A weekend spent suspended. Monday: another CT
and EEG, insertion of a feeding tube, PIC line, port

for dialysis. Some doctors stopped meeting my eyes,
rubbed my shoulders even when I flinched. I started

telling you it was okay to go, that I could learn to manage
on my own, that your mom and grandmother were waiting

with my dad to welcome you—and if those weren't things
that I'd believed before, I needed to believe them then.

Once the neurologist I never met agreed your brain was gone,
nurses unsnaked tubes and turned off your alarms. They warned

it might take days for you to wind completely down,
your lungs inflating on their own but to the wrong capacity

and rhythm. Because I didn't think you'd die if I was there,
I asked E. to drive me home, sit with me while I ate.

Then there was nothing left to wait for anymore.
I grew up surrounded by sirens and urgency, the promise

help was coming soon. But when I went to see you
the last time—your skin already cool and mottling,

your chest completely still under its blue gown,
your absence finally fact and not just likelihood—

the emergency was less your death than how my world
changed, how my life could go on without you in it.

Preparing to Leave the Hospital:
A Beginner's Guide

Especially after a long stay ending
in your husband's death, you may feel
unready to go home. You may wish
you had a discharge plan to tell you what
comes next, how you should shape your days
around the loss that you feel swallowed by.
The first day of your widowhood,
you may welcome the distraction
of small tasks—throwing away his pills,
cleaning out the fridge, asking a coworker
you barely know to drive you to the hospital
because you left his slippers, sweater,
underwear, then to the funeral home
to arrange cremation. When placing
desperate, grieving calls to friends, it's best
to spread your need around so no one
gets burned out. Try not to be upset
when people don't pick up, then send you
breezy texts about the trips they're taking,
their busy weeks at work, how they hope
you're okay and promise to call soon.

You may hate being told to take care
of yourself, then wish the advice were more
detailed. How much should you sleep,
what are you supposed to eat, how many
blankets will you need before you're warm?
Is drinking every day acceptable
if it's just beer and never more than two?
How often should you lose your train
of thought, wander the house unsure of what
your purpose is? Ordinary chores—
taking out the trash, folding laundry,

writing checks for services insurance
doesn't cover—may feel impossibly hard.
When declining coffee, lunch, movies
meant to cheer you up, don't mention panic
rising in your chest, how small and scared
you often feel. If you're concerned
that you're not acting like yourself,
remember—the self that you are now
isn't the same as who you were before.

Your grief may be complicated by regret
you weren't a better caregiver and advocate.
You may suspect you could've stopped
his death if you'd done more research,
insisted on specialists and transfer
somewhere else, been on guard against mistakes
and negligence. And yet you may also find
you crave the safety of the hospital,
the routines and relationships you formed,
the comfort of the cafeteria, workers
who blessed you when you paid. Driving past
the complex on your way somewhere else,
you may be tempted to pull in, make your way
through the lobby, halls you know so well.
You may feel some vital part of you
is stranded in the ICU, that everything
that happened there is somehow happening still.

DEAR JOAN DIDION,

when I first read your memoir of your husband's death,
mine was still alive. Though he'd been very ill that year,

I never thought my widowhood would come so soon,
that when it did I'd turn to you less for advice than company.

Like you, I'm obsessed with chronology, narrative I need
to understand. Afraid I might forget, I went back and filled

the blank days of my calendar with tests and surgeries,
times he'd been discharged and readmitted, morning

he was resuscitated, night he finally died. I can't quit
picking at the language people used. Doctors said

*metabolic derangement, hemostatic instability, la belle
indifférence.* The funeral director: *He's in our care now,*

as though care were still possible. I insist my husband
died instead of *was lost, passed on* or *away,*

because I need to practice stating facts. Like you,
I'm aware that I'm not always rational. I haven't closed

his bank accounts, put the cable in my name or donated
the shoes he wore the most. For several weeks,

I thought about returning to the ICU to prove
he wasn't there. At first I didn't go because I was too tired,

because I worried nurses would remember me and think
I was unwell, and eventually the urge faded away.

I never realize I've been bargaining until after the deadline
passes: If I survive Thanksgiving, finish the semester,

make it through Christmas; if I act strong, hold on without
falling apart—my husband will come home, tell me

I've done so well he'll never leave again. Each time
my fantasies collapse, my disappointment is outweighed

by shame at the cliché. Because, like you, I thought
there had to be answers somewhere, I've read studies

on grief, discovered most assumptions aren't supported
by research. When friends say they're relieved

I'm writing, I want to clarify it doesn't help that much.
His death feels too big to understand in words,

but I know I'll keep trying. Joan, I don't expect you
to reply. You must get these letters all the time,

and I don't think we're destined to grow close.
But there is one thing I wonder: whether you, like me,

believe grief hasn't altered who you are so much
as it's intensified the aspects of yourself—those

you're proudest of, those you wish you could deny—
that you already recognize. If I say I didn't take much

comfort from your book, please know I'm not blaming you.
I've always craved more comfort than the world supplies.

Letter I Don't Know Where to Send

I keep your ashes on a shelf but I sometimes pretend
you're still crossing the street or stepping off the bus
with a canvas bag of Walgreens bounty—batteries,

mouthwash, candy, Venus razors you got almost-free.
Or maybe you're back in Columbia bouncing at a club
or Antler party the way you were the night I saw you

the first time, when you threw a guy I knew—gently,
I came to understand—against a car because he was
a mouthy jerk. Or you're in Lincoln at the barbershop

where all the coaches went, in Columbus advising
your fraternity. We lived in so many college towns
that all had the same heart—football, bars, bands,

students gathered at the Union or the Quad. Even
in Providence, which you didn't get to know that well,
you went to campus yard-sale day and loaned

your Tide pen to a kid dressed for an interview.
When people ask what you were like, I always tell
the same two stories: how the night we met, you offered

to get me in the Blue Note any time and laughed when I
insulted you, how after we left together we never
were apart. And how, during last summer's long drive east,

I told you about the young gas-station couple rationing
their cash and you remembered their Missouri plates,
dog in the back seat, said you wished we'd given them

something because it's hard not to have enough
money, sleep, people to call in an emergency.
We only talked about our deaths in joking ways,

but when I asked your idea of heaven for a poem,
cornbread and fishing made the final draft. I wish
the times that I feel lost made us more equal

than they do. If it's true you exist somewhere,
you must know where that is, and also know
I'm still here in the place you were but won't return.

TEACHING HOSPITAL

In the ICU, the student doctors came in flocks
so large the white wings of their coats
obscured my husband's bed. The patterns
of their flights were unpredictable. Sometimes
they came to our room first, sometimes last
or in the middle. While I weighed how long
I could stay against what I might learn,
I watched them gather at the nurses' station,
laughing, pecking at laptop keys, conferring
in low voices I worked hard to overhear.

Despite having seen every season of *ER*,
I didn't always understand who was the most
advanced, whose opinion I could trust
and whose I wanted checked. My favorite
resident was tall and serious, more senior
than the rest. The day my husband
was resuscitated, I heard him volunteer
to tell *the wife*, which is how I introduced myself
when he walked up. After that he was
the one I looked for on the floor, the one
who described tests and what would happen
next, the one I knew would tell the truth
about how sick my husband was.

The last few days before he died, the flock
of doctors thinned to just a few, and I couldn't help
but wonder why the students didn't come,
if they were trying to respect our privacy
or had been reassigned. I hoped they had better
models for death than the attending
who turned his face away as he announced
that though my husband's brain was dead,

his kidney would recover given time.
Once I said I wanted life support removed,
he disappeared and left us with my resident.

I don't know what my husband's body
may have taught, if his case was textbook
or unusual, if the students thought of us
at all after their flock moved on. I know
I learned less during his death than I expected:
that I'd run out of things to say beside his bed;
that every day I'd want to eat and walk
the dog, wear socks that didn't clash;
that even with a week of warning, the final
stillness of his chest would feel like a surprise.

Parallel Grief

When the nurses said my dad was dying,
we rushed into his room. My mom
pressed her palm against his chest, said
He's already gone. I wasn't sure
but trusted she knew best. Up until
the very end, he could follow conversation
and respond, tell my mom he wanted
to go home. She says if she'd known
how close to death he was, she would've
wheeled him to the car instead of waiting
on more tests, doctors to interpret them.
I'm glad she didn't try the ninety-minute
drive, steep porch stairs he'd built
himself, but I understand her guilt.

I wasn't with my husband when he died,
had no idea his heart had stopped until
the doctor called. By the time I swore
I'd take him home, I wasn't sure
if he could hear, already meant his ashes
and not him. It was my fault he didn't
have a death more like my dad's,
that we'd moved so far away his family
couldn't come. Every time we moved
it was my fault, and every time he said
it sounded fun, talked me out of my doubt.

The first day he felt sick I blamed
bad takeout, snacks while I was sleeping.
Even when he threw up in the night,
even the next morning as I tried to find
an urgent care with him not helping me at all,
I thought his stomach hurt because of heat
and heavy lifting, the stress of our big move.
My mom says every time she thought

my dad was sick, his excuses made sense—
he'd done too much outside in high
humidity, overeaten or not slept enough.
Maybe that's what he believed,
or maybe he suspected something worse
and didn't want his fears confirmed.

I stayed with my mom the first week
of her widowhood. I thought while I
was helping her, she was teaching me
how to survive a husband's death.
I didn't know that in ten weeks
I'd be a widow, too, or that the help
I'd want the most I'd never have again.

I've never really told my mom the story
of my husband's death, the ways it overlaps
with Dad's, regret I feel for reasons
much like hers. And I don't know
what she's not telling me, what I've misheard
or taken the wrong way. Twice a week
we talk about the weather, work,
household tasks we've tackled
or are putting off. The pain that we're
both in, worries we're somehow to blame,
aren't things we want to share.

Grudges: A Partial List

Hospital personnel who got my husband's history wrong,
assumed he'd always been as sick as he got in their care

and that it was our fault. The nurse with frosted eyeshadow
who made a snipping gesture near his toes and only knew

three things she kept repeating. The intern who suggested
ICU when we'd thought he was getting well.

At the time I was upset by his eagerness, but now
I'm furious he didn't fight, sign the transfer right away.

The case manager who tried to discharge him too soon,
then shipped him to a rehab with no bed. The resident

who seemed too chipper and well-groomed to be competent,
specialist who came to my unconscious husband's room

to brag that he'd predicted a decline. The social worker
with her pamphlets about aftercare, shock when I walked out.

The other family on the floor the day he died, their greasy
sandwiches and need to share about their mom. The funeral

home that put my husband's ashes in a tote bag printed
with their name, student who missed class my first day back

because, he said, of hardships I could never comprehend.
The man who made me promise to *Stay strong*, woman

who wrote *I hope your load is lightening* after just
three weeks. Even my mom, who said she'd suspected

I'd be widowed young. My husband, who swore he didn't
want to die but then did anyway, who left me with

an apartment that's too big, a dog that gets up in the night
to see if he's come home, questions I'll never get an answer to:

if I gave up and took his life support too soon, what I'm
supposed to do with all his things, if he heard or cared about

what I said at the end. Myself, for every time I dreaded
driving to the hospital, left sooner than I'd planned and wished

I hadn't gone. My embarrassment when he needed a walker,
wheelchair, potty beside the bed. Every time I looked

at him and thought, *Is this the life we're going to have?*
For not realizing he might die until he started to.

LETTER I MAY NEVER FINISH

I made myself use up the tissues
from the hospital though they were scratchy
and too small. When my hummus
was recalled, I almost ate it anyway,
cried when I checked the UPCs,
requested money back. I know
it's a bad idea to just keep piling papers
on your desk. I gave away
your graphing calculator, put your planner
in a box, but left the feather
with its faded black-tan stripes,
the right leg of an action figure
I found in the street.

You could've changed the bulb
above the sink by barely stretching,
would've cringed to see me standing
on the counter courting vertigo.
It took me a month to stop
the DVR from recording your shows,
another month to delete what
you'd missed. I wonder sometimes
what you would've done if I had died
instead, if you'd try to find homes
for all my clothes instead of just
calling a truck, how long you'd wait
to change my pillowcases, give away
my coffee cups and peanut butter.

If you'd close my study door
or leave it open, sit down at my desk
and hold my pen. If the news
you needed me to hear would seem
too trivial to tell anyone else.
If you'd whisper it out loud

or write it down the way I do.
When you died, I was sure
we'd said everything that mattered.
The problem is that things keep happening,
things only you could care about
or grasp the meaning of.

DEAR MARK DOTY,

I don't expect you to remember this,
but ten years ago in Omaha my husband and I met you
at a writing conference dinner. He didn't realize who you were
until the car ride home—he'd just seen two empty seats,

been glad you laughed with him and weren't stuck up.
I only had a week to think about his death before
it was a fact. Watching his unsteady breaths supported
by a respirator, I sometimes felt that I was dying, too,

or else already had. I moved and ate and took up space
but was so full of grief my self had gone away. Like yours,
my body hurt in ways I recognized as metaphors.
For months the muscles in my chest pressed hard

against my lungs, left me dizzy and stunned. Because my neck
and shoulders didn't ache if I looked down, when I walked
the dog I picked up pennies, pencils I could use despite
bite marks, erasers ground to the ferrule. Like you,

I'm not sure what it means to let my husband go, if that's
something I want or think is possible. I've cleaned out
his closet and his desk, taken his ashes to the place
where they belong, all things I'm told mean moving on,

and yet each day is marked by absence most of all.
He always loved the world more than I did. He knew
the neighbors' names and made friends on the bus,
made lists of things he meant to learn and see. Sometimes

I try to be generous like him. Then I wonder if waving cars
into traffic counts, making eye contact with strangers
when I'd rather not. Mark, if we're ever introduced again,
I won't retell the night this letter started with. If you said

you remembered us—remembered him—I'd assume
you were lying to be kind, while if you confessed
you didn't, I couldn't help being upset. I'm not bitter
all the time but like you I wish more people would admit

how often comfort fails or doesn't last, how without him
to share it with, even beauty brings me pain. Mark, I hope
my husband died in the same radiance you sensed
when Wally did. I just find it hard to hold on to that light.

SECTION TWO

ON DAYS I DON'T THINK I'LL DIE OF GRIEF,

I don't wake up in tears from dreams I don't
remember. I don't have to hold my coffee
with both hands or wear an extra sweater
to stop shivering, don't have to write down
when I need to leave and what to take for lunch.
I don't have to remind myself my racing
thoughts are only thoughts and nothing bad
has happened—or at least nothing else—
and even if it has I can't prevent every disaster.
I don't turn up the shower until it scalds
my skin, don't forget if I've already washed
my hair. I don't feel like my clothes belong
to someone else, don't worry I can't see
my sweater's stained, heels scuffed beyond
what polish covers. I don't look for my keys
and find them in my hand, don't drive
to work wishing I could hide behind black veils,
take to my bed with fainting fits and fevers.
I don't cross the parking lot—breath short,
shoulders sinking to my knees—as though
I'm moving underwater, don't assume
the hallway pleasantries I stumble through
are proof my colleagues are discussing me.
In my classroom, I don't have to keep
checking the syllabus and date,
don't count how many weeks it's been.
When yet another student poem claims
that once your heart's been *torn, shattered,*
or *destroyed,* your life is over, too, and all
that's left is loneliness until you die, I don't
feel tempted to display the widow card
my students don't all know I have, explain
that you can be in pain and hold a job,
grocery shop and dress correctly for the weather.
After class, I don't drive home in a panic,

every red light making me feel later, then realize
I'm not headed to the hospital. I don't open
a beer before I hang my coat, don't take it
with me when I get the mail, change back
into pajamas I don't wash. I don't
surprise myself by crying when I thought
I was okay, don't scroll through my contacts
for someone to call, don't resist because
voicemail might mean that person's busy
or avoiding me. I don't suspect my friends
have stopped consulting me about their own
concerns because they think their needs
will never measure up, because I can't be trusted
or depended on. I don't eat dinner
hunched over my plate, don't stare at TV
I don't care about while wondering
which choices I'll regret, what damage
I'll have to correct once my right mind returns.
I don't brush my teeth and go to bed
at an absurdly early hour feeling
utterly exhausted and aware I shouldn't be.
On days I don't think I'll die of grief,
I'm not afraid that everyone I know
is grateful they're not me, that the changes
I hate most—in my self and the world—
are permanent and only for the worse.

THE ANGRY WIDOWS

don't drink tea.
They want to burn down all the Hallmark stores,
smash every angel figurine. They shrug away
from your embrace, think your prayers
are useless and too late. The angry widows
dump lasagna in the trash, pour soup
down the drain and eat a cheeseburger
instead, then lick grease off the plate.

The angry widows don't wear black
and are unlikely to collapse. They cut off
cars in traffic, storm out of stores
with too-long lines. The angry widows
don't want therapy. Support groups
make them spit. They hate hot baths,
candles, and anything designed
to increase mindfulness. Their minds
are what they wish they could escape.

If the angry widows walked into a bar,
they wouldn't sit in corners crying
pretty tears. They'd load the jukebox
with their favorite songs, sing too loud
and dance while holding drinks.
If you asked them to settle down,
they'd want to step outside. You'd end up
with your pool cue snapped in half,
your nose and windshield broken,
tires slashed. If the police were called,
the angry widows wouldn't weep
and go home with a warning. Instead
they'd swing until the cuffs clicked on.

The angry widows never watch the news.
As far as they're concerned, the worst
forecast has come true. They know
you need them to grieve with grace
and fortitude, but they have none to give.
Even when the angry widows seem
content, inside they're smoldering.
They may never hurt the world as much
as it's hurt them, but they're willing to try.

Holiday Letter

A month after you died, I made pie
and green bean casserole—no potatoes,
gravy, meat. A coworker invited me
to dinner, but I stayed home so I could cry
remembering: J. carving the turkey
I hated to cook, T. coaching the Cowboys
through the screen, the year
we used our neighbor's oven, too,
and also years we feasted on our own,
ate in our pajamas and declared it good.

Ignoring Christmas seemed sadder
than having it. I lugged the village totes
upstairs, prepared to put out
our favorite pieces—pub, school,
post office and fire station—and donate
the rest. I didn't know I'd also find
the toy train from your childhood,
your mom's ashtray and purse,
proof you'd learned to pack the way
I do, without wasting any space.
Christmas Day, I didn't cook or feel
as bad as I'd anticipated. I opened
my few gifts, imagined you and Dad
sitting in the basement in Missouri,
him with the presents I signed
your name to—whiskey, lottery tickets,
bikini calendar—you with your glasses on
to check how much he'd won.

New Year's Eve, I went to bed
at nine, slept until the dog woke up
afraid of fireworks I hadn't heard.
I gave him Benadryl, pressed
my hand against his back until

his vigilance relaxed. Even though
the Patriots played in the Super Bowl,
I didn't watch a single down.
I made soup from potatoes we'd bought
in September—your last trip to the store,
the day your death began. S. and K.
both wrote to reminisce about parties
we'd had, prizes you gave if we guessed
right about the game. I always
said yes to *Will there be a safety?*
but this year I'm not sure.

One morning on my way to work,
an ad for Shari's Berries upset me
so much you would've suggested
pulling over. Just before your coma
in October, you'd apologized
you hadn't put my birthday order in,
and I'd almost confessed
that I'd grown sick of their hard
chocolate shells, fruit always
overripe yet sour. The 14th
was easy in comparison. I quoted
Margaret Atwood's "February,"
pretended not to notice hearts.

Even the first big snow felt like
something you were missing.
Not just schools but the entire state
shut down. I wanted to joke about
driving to Wendy's for a cup of chili
the way my dad did during blizzards,
remind you of the day that you and he—
lead car in our convoy of two—
insisted we stop for lunch
while snow hid the twisting blacktop
to my parents' house, how Mom

and I cursed both of you each time
my tires slid. After a whole day passed
without our driveway being plowed,
I finally went outside. You would've
left neater edges next to the garage,
but I just wanted to back out.

I haven't seen *SportsCenter* since
you died, but I'll miss filling out
my bracket for March Madness,
eating at Applebee's during the early
daytime rounds. I was too stunned
to notice Halloween, so I'm wearing
those socks now, neon bats
and candy corn I won't replace
when they wear out. People warned me
holidays would hurt, but I hadn't known
they'd hurt in such specific ways,
or that we'd had so many marked
by just us two: *Survivor* night
and spring-break shopping day,
weekends I declared the kitchen
closed. I feel better than I did
four months ago, but without you,
most days are something
I observe instead of celebrate.

Dear Grief,

I wish you wouldn't text
my friends when you've been drinking,
call the landlord to complain about the heat,
slow drain in the bathroom sink. I don't know
why he talks to you—your name's not on
the lease. You make me pay for everything,
not just rent and utilities but takeout you let
molder in the fridge, clothes you buy online
and claim are gifts although they're never
in my size. You borrow books and drown them
in the shower, scratch up my car and fill my bed
with bowls of oatmeal you've abandoned,
tissues I won't touch. I'm sure you're the reason
I feel sick: fevers, headaches, swollen joints
and pressure in my chest. I've adapted
to the stomach pain but not the vertigo,
how my brain senses subtext even from
my friends. When I try to go out for air,
an hour on my own, you insist on coming, too,
stand so close your shadow swallows mine.

Grief, you're the worst roommate I've ever had.
I hate the way you hog hot water, play awful
music on repeat and set my clocks ten minutes
slow to make me scramble. And I hate
the questions and regrets you save for 4 a.m.,
whispers that keep me wide awake. And yet
no matter how upset with you I get, I admit
it hasn't all been terrible. I like it when you sit
and listen to my stories, how you don't say
I'm making you too sad or try to drag me
off the couch. You just ask if I'm warm enough,
hand me the remote and let me pick the shows.
Grief, I can't afford for you to stay forever,
but you don't have to move out right away.

Malpractice Letter

Before you died, when friends asked
if I was happy with the hospital, treatment
you received, I always felt defensive
saying yes, as though I should've done
research, had reasons for going there
besides a doctor's office told us to
and it was near our house. Now when
they ask if I have plans to sue, I'm not sure
if they really think I should or if
they mean they're shocked and sorry.

You didn't have to ask your doctors much
because you knew I'd come to clarify
and question, make them explain
until I understood. When the hospital
last tried to send you home, I yelled
at your case manager, demanded proof
that you were well. Discharge
to a rehab center felt like victory,
but the trip there made you so sick
you went right back to the ER.
If you'd been angry then, I would've
argued blame could wait, but you
were grateful you were readmitted.

By the end, your case had grown
so complicated, your body failing
in so many ways, I believe your doctors
did the best they could, made choices
that made sense but didn't save you.
I've wondered if you were presented
at an M&M, if the resident I liked
so much took your death with him
when his rotation ended. Even though
he was the one who'd asked, I refused

an autopsy because doctors had done
enough. I didn't care what they could
learn, what would count as evidence
in a lawsuit I wasn't planning.

Sometimes I worry I should want
to sue—out of outrage or devotion—
but it doesn't seem worth the years
I'd spend reliving your last month.
I'd be asked to estimate your pain
and future earnings, how strong
our marriage was, and also have to fear
who their defense would blame—
doctors in other states or us for carelessness.
And even if we proved our case,
proved mistakes or negligence, I'd have
to live with knowing that despite
the hours I'd spent by your bed
I hadn't noticed you were being killed.
I know nothing I could win
would make us whole again.

User Agreement

Your widow card is active right away.
There's no need to sign the back,
select a PIN or suffer the fine print.
No one tracks the balance on your card,
and only sympathetic interest will accrue.
In lieu of an annual fee, there will be
one-time funeral expenses and the income
reduction you already dread. Accepted
nearly everywhere, your widow card
allows you to avoid the dentist
and social events, excuses sudden tears
that soak your sleeve. Some widows turn
to their cards sparingly in order
to show strength, others as a first resort.
Regardless of your wishes, special treatment
may occur: You may be subjected
to condolences you'd rather avoid, asked
intrusive questions or perceived as weak.
Any resulting awkwardness is not your fault
and may be eased by further applications
of the card itself. While it has its greatest value
in the first six months, it never expires,
regardless of remarriage or time
since its last use. Incidents of theft
and fraud are rare, though people may attempt
to speak or act on your behalf, claim
greater closeness than in fact exists.
We promise our office won't bother
you again. Nor is it possible for you
to contact us. You'll have to find out
for yourself how best to use your card,
behave as the bereaved. We understand
that in the midst of your raw grief,
the receipt of your widow card can't help
but be unwelcome. But given that

your deepest wish—to have your partner
back—can never be fulfilled, we urge you
to accept the benefits your card can bring.
However small such comforts seem,
at least they're guaranteed.

ALTERNATE ENDINGS

In a Lifetime movie about hope,
I'd stay beside my husband's bed,
refuse to eat or sleep until I'd said
the magic words that made
his eyelids flutter, fingers move
in mine. I'd fight his doctors
for more tests, treatments still
in trial phase. The therapy I'd learn
to give at home, second job
I'd have to take, would pay off
with the miracle of him saying
my name, reaching to touch my face.

In a Lifetime movie about loss,
I'd be with my husband
when he died, tender one last kiss
to his chapped lips while his heartbeat
stuttered and went still.
At the funeral, I wouldn't fling myself
across his coffined chest or faint
beside his grave, but my apparent
bravery would give way to wine bottles,
my body spilled on marble floors.

In a Lifetime movie about wrongful
death, I'd pore over his charts,
marking crucial facts with flags
and highlighters, be sorrowful
but fierce each time I was deposed.
Having exposed years of negligence
and careful cover-ups, I'd force
his doctors to confess not just
mistakes but crimes, offer me
a check I'd righteously refuse
or give to someone else.

In a Lifetime movie about secrets,
when I went through his desk
for paperwork, the watch I wanted
his best friend to have, I'd find
assets I didn't recognize. Slowly
I'd learn our life had been a lie,
my husband at best a bigamist
but probably a thief or contract killer,
kingpin dealing drugs or guns.
I'd endanger myself to uncover
the truth, meet a handsome
federal agent who made me feel safe.

In a Lifetime movie about justice,
I'd be a murderess who caused
my husband's death in order to inherit,
to protect my pornographic past
or revel in the sympathy
that follows loss. Brought to trial
by the teamwork of an attentive
neighbor, gruff detective who liked
breaking rules, I'd dress my guilt
in pearls and a cardigan but wind up
wearing orange as my pursuers wed.

In a Lifetime movie about resilience,
I'd spiral briefly into partying
and stupid sex, then rent a cottage
on an empty beach, launch myself
into the wilderness, discover
Buddhism while traveling overseas.
I'd come home determined to
open a bakery, daycare for dogs
or bookstore crammed with poetry.
Or I'd revive old dreams
of earning an advanced degree,
taking up trapeze or marathons.

In a Lifetime movie about finding love
again, one day I'd slowly slide off
my rings, then walk along a tree-lined
street, admire snow or daffodils.
A few terrible dates would lead to
a meet-cute with a handyman, owner
of the local pub, dog-lover whose leash
tangled with mine. At first afraid
to risk my heart again, I'd slowly
surrender to his patient charm.

In a Lifetime movie, the plot
might be disjointed or absurd,
but it would have a clear trajectory,
teasers hinting what would happen
next. My husband might still die,
but as long as it wasn't my fault
my awful grief would be resolved
before the audience got bored,
my suffering rewarded with
the ending I deserved.

Dear Joyce Carol Oates,

I'm grateful I reread your memoir
when I did, found ways our stories overlapped
although they're not a perfect match.
The accident my husband and I had
was nowhere near as serious as yours—
no airbags, injuries except stiff necks
and shivering. Afterward, when I described
our car flying off the icy interstate
into the median, *We could've died*
was true but mostly for effect—
I never felt we lived on borrowed time.

Like you, I wonder if I should've known
how sick he was before the doctors did,
if I trusted the wrong hospital, was foolish
to believe he would get well. My husband
was a charming patient just like yours.
Doctors enjoyed his jokes but he still died.
I, too, refused the autopsy because
I didn't see how it could help, then opted
for cremation, decisions that would make
malpractice harder to pursue, though
also like you I don't think anyone's at fault.

Like you, I hurried back to teaching
to help fill my days, help me escape
the thoughts I couldn't stop: the long walk
through the lobby to the ICU, corner
by the double doors where I waited for news,
my husband's body in the bed I'd spent
hours beside. So far, no one has said
he chose to die because he just got tired,
but some people insist he'd expected his death,
others that they weren't surprised.

Like you, I often try to prove how well
I'm holding up so friends can worry less,
be reassured they, too, could survive
a loss like this. Even if my pride would let me
say the words, no one wants to hear
I'm actually a mess. I never had a basilisk
I needed to avoid, but there were times
I wished I'd kept my husband's pills,
knew who would take my dog.

Joyce, I was glad when you stopped suffering
so much, glad when you met someone
because I hope that I'll remarry, too,
but my favorite part is what you say
on your last page. If it's true
a widow's most important task—
at least for her first year—
is making sure she stays alive,
I'm happy to report I'm halfway there.

Discharge Letter

I knew the third time was too soon,
then was afraid I felt that way
because I was so tired. All weekend
you refused to eat or watch the game,
look through mail I'd sorted
on your desk. Instead you stared
at rain that made you shiver, asked me
for heat although it wasn't cold.
Sunday before bed you swallowed
your new pills, complained my light
was bothering your eyes. I slept
so hard I didn't hear you getting up,
calling my name to say you needed
the ER. By then we'd been
to two, so I asked you to choose
while I got dressed, found shoes
to force onto your swollen feet.

The nurse who took you back
told me I couldn't come. I tried
to read but kept jerking awake afraid
of where I was, what might be
happening behind those double doors.
When I saw you again, you were
more theirs than mine—IV,
heart monitor, white blanket smoothed
over your chest, your face finally
relaxing as pain meds kicked in.
I'm sure I held your hand
but don't remember what we said,
if I sat in the curtained cubicle
while they took you for tests or if
that was a different trip. It was clear
you had to stay, clear I was
in the way and that you wanted rest.

Outside, I was amazed the Walgreens
was still lit, that there were other drivers
out at 1 a.m. I didn't really sleep
but also didn't call to ask whether
you'd been admitted yet.
I knew the wait on hold would be
excruciating, that it might be
afternoon before you had a room,
wanted me to witness how you were.

October used to be my favorite month.
Now each glance at the calendar
reminds me how long you had left
last year, which floor your room
was on, what doctors thought
was wrong that wasn't
the whole truth. I don't regret
not knowing you weren't coming home.
That night I still believed
if I put you in the right hands,
you'd heal enough to only need
the care that I could give.

DEAR GAIL GODWIN,

I read *Evenings at Five* because
I knew you were a widow, too,
but I was still surprised to find
a character I felt such kinship with.
Like Christina, I refuse to see
my husband as a saint and sometimes
miss habits we bickered over:
chewed bits of fingernail embedded
in the couch where he dozed
watching loud TV, tantrums
he threw when I accused him
of not listening. Like her,
I find the most ordinary items—
rose-handled spoon that he ate
soup and ice cream with, ceramic
moose I never cared much for—
have taken on the weight
of talismans. Evenings bother me
much less than afternoons,
but I, too, find sitting with
the absence that my husband left
both comforting and necessary.
I know our life together won't go on
in the same way, but there are parts
of it that don't feel finished yet.

Even though I know it's dangerous
to treat fiction like memoir,
I wondered if you'd ever had
a night like Christina does,
one where you told your husband
everything you needed him
to know, then felt a kind of peace.
If that's true, I'm glad for you,
but for me the final chapters

moved too fast. I wondered
how long Christina's relief
would really last, if she'd need
another Scotch so she could sleep,
if the next evening at five
she'd realize her sadness
hadn't changed. Gail, I had no idea
my grief would stay so messy
for so long, that I'd try on
so many ways to be a widow
without finding one that fit.
Please know my complaint
about your book is based
in jealousy—Christina gets
the closure I keep hoping for
but can't be sure exists.

Interment Letter

The cemetery smelled like the ones
my family used to mow—hot grass
and damp red clay, a hint of honeysuckle
blooming somewhere out of sight.
While your uncles dug the hole,
I walked the dog in circles so
he couldn't help. My arms and ankles
itched. I worried about ticks, how much
I was sweating in my long gray pants,
shirt I wear to meetings when I want
to feel grown-up. When Cousin T.
asked how much space you'd need,
I held out the heavy plastic cube
I'd lived with since last fall.
He offered to put you in the ground,
but I did it myself. While your aunt
read the shepherd psalm, I picked at clay
climbing my wrist. Then we used
our hands to fill the hole, replant clumps
of grass we hoped the rain would save.

I didn't cry because I have enough
already, because I was focused
on details to tell you later: Your family
dug the hole. When I hugged P.,
he squeezed my hips. Mom tripped
and fell into a stone that could've
cracked her skull. Your cousin asked
if I'd saved any ashes for myself,
planned to be buried beside you—
and also if it bothered me the grave
I'd promised you was far away
from where I live. I didn't answer him
because it seemed too soon to say.

WHAT ARE DAYS FOR?

After Phillip Larkin and Julie Bruck

My first answer was a lie. I said
To walk the dog and thought
that was enough, ignored the days
I'm glad it rains, that it's too hot
or cold for us to leave the yard.
I should've said *To take care of,*
admitted that I sometimes fail.

My husband wasn't sick
most of our marriage, but when he was
I scrambled eggs, counted pills
and wiped up blood, complained
about the needs he needed me
to meet. Last fall, he was too weak
to stand up in the shower,
so I put a lawn chair in the tub
and washed his hair with no-tears
dog shampoo, my concern
mixed with pride at a problem solved.

After my dad died, my mom
was in so much pain I worried
she wouldn't survive. Every time
we talked, I'd hang up and tell
my husband I was scared.
Then he died, too, and even though
I tried to reach my mom through
my own grief, I know sometimes
I quit too soon, just like the day
I tried to save a student stumbling
on the stairs, then walked away
while someone else asked if
she was okay, helped her sit down
so she could catch her breath.

When it was clear my husband
wasn't going to wake up, his nurses
offered coffee, juice, the remote
for his TV. The day after he died,
I kept the dog's appointment
at the vet, brought records
I'd requested from Wisconsin.

I let my *Service Engine* light stay on
for months, trusting the mechanic
with my father's name who'd told me
in September I wouldn't break down.
In February, I sat at the dealership
while my dad's voice gave a lecture
I deserved—how could I have put off
the repairs so long, risked making
damage worse. That spring, I only learned
my friend was ill after she'd been
discharged. Before, she would've
called if not when symptoms
started, then at least from the ER.

When I'm told to look after myself,
I always say I will, but making sure
I eat and sleep and shower doesn't feel
that satisfying. I'd rather focus
on the car, the dog, the friends
who still ask my advice, my mom
who I can only tend long-distance.
Without enough to take care of,
I might forget what days are for.

SECTION THREE

Dear Sandra M. Gilbert,

I opened *Death's Door* so you could tell me
what the figure of the Widow meant.
It's appealing to believe I'm seen as having

power, *privileged access* to the *mysteries
of death*, but like you I seem to inspire
much less awe than awkwardness.

Even when my insides churn with rage
and sorrow, my *unseemly screams*
stay stuck inside my throat, my *morbid*

glamour limited to looking tired. I won't
assume writing your books made you
feel better. My poems never do except

that I'm so used to sitting at my desk
that sometimes when I'm thinking very hard,
my sadness seems to weigh a little less.

Sandra, I can't help but wonder how you feel
about the books you made out of and from
your husband's death, if you pretend

they don't exist or flip through them
and find phrases you repeated because
you were stuck, confessions you regret

or don't remember making. I won't ask
whether all your words were worth it
in the end. I have to think they were.

But I wish you could tell me how it felt
to realize that despite how hard you'd tried,
there were still things you'd written wrong

or been afraid to say. Sandra, I know
I won't need to write my husband's death forever.
But I also can't imagine having said enough.

MY DEAD HUSBAND

                   never wore a watch
or was ready to leave on time. He thought
I should wash my car more often, hated
cell phones except when he borrowed mine.
Even with the window open, his showers
built up so much steam the smoke detector
chirped. He needed more sleep than me,
ate food I wouldn't touch—white bread,
bologna, frozen pizzas tasting of cardboard.
Although his size could make him seem
intimidating, he made friends everywhere
because he was so kind. He'd love
that people talk about his jokes, how warm
his smile was. He wouldn't want me
to point out that sometimes he was lonely, too,
loaded down with worries he only told
to me. My dead husband had amazing legs.
He was great at *Wheel of Fortune*, math,
and understanding puns on license plates.
He never put the scissors back where they
belonged. He left the lids off condiments,
left mud and dirty dishes all over the house.
At least twice a week he lost his keys
and temper, apologized by being silent
until I gave in. Every night he watched
the local news and told me what I'd missed.
He also always did the decorating. He didn't
have the greatest taste, but it was better
than blank walls. He clipped coupons
and read the grocery ad, kept a notebook
of products I used—tampons, lotion,
deodorant—so he'd buy the right brands.
When I mention my dead husband
in the present tense, I make myself go back
and clarify. He'd prefer I use a euphemism—

late, departed, passed—would say
it isn't nice to like when people flinch.
I'm not as angry as I was right after
he died, but I no longer let him vote
at family meetings. Sometimes I'm jealous
that he'll never have to change, reshape
his life all on his own. My dead husband
couldn't stand for me to be upset.
No matter what the problem was,
he'd swear we'd be okay, make jokes
to show at least we had each other.
I can't imagine what he'd say right now.

GRIEF LOGIC

After Louise Glück

My mom says parents shouldn't live with
      their grown kids, and also that she doesn't
            want to get much older. I can gauge

her loneliness by how often she calls,
      mine by how quick I am to answer.
            One night when she was ill—a migraine

caused by tension in her damaged neck—
      she saw a dead mouse on her porch,
            then spotted a whole pile of them, tails

tucked around gray bodies. Too weak
      to sweep them away, she stayed awake
            convinced they'd been left by a neighbor

she'd upset. In the morning, the mice
      she'd seen were curled maple leaves—
            and yet she still felt stung by the insult

she'd imagined. If I tried to describe what
      I was making of my grief, my first answer
            would probably be *a mess*, my second

that I'm trying to make sense. When Mom
      told me about the mice, I didn't let myself
            confess they've been on my porch, too,

describe how slow I was to realize what
      they really were, resolve the hurt that I,
            like her, had sentenced myself to. Instead

I asked why someone wouldn't simply
            slash her tires or tear up her flowers,
                        then rolled my eyes when she sighed

in response. Even though I know it isn't
            kind, sometimes I try to reason with
                        my mother's grief because I can't with mine.

Dear Sheryl Sandberg,

I agree *the weather has been weird*
with all this rain and death, that books
on grief have awful titles. *Option B*
isn't the worst I've heard although
it makes me think of birth control,
those logic puzzles I won't try to solve.
I love how you describe the elephant
that followed you around, how people
managed to ignore its size and smell,
the shovel you stood ready with.
I, too, sometimes feel that I've become
a ghost, both *frightening and invisible*.
And while I've never wanted to lean in,
I laughed out loud when you confessed
that simply standing up was hard enough.

But I find I can't forgive you for
the ocean metaphors and emphasis
on growth, how you dreamed up
a version of the footprints story—
your friends walking behind in case
you fell—that annoys me more
than the original. I hate the way
you cherry-pick research, name-drop
celebrities, end every chapter trying
to inspire. And most of all I hate
how even though you mention anger
early on it quickly goes away,
how you insist resilience can be learned
if I'll just put the effort in.

Sheryl, I admit that I don't always
reach for joy. Often I resort
to ice cream and TV, mysteries

I can read in a day and then forget
forever. Recently a friend accused me
of refusing to rejoin the world,
said she'd decided to back off and stop
playing psychologist. Despite being
furious—because I was hurt and also
scared she had a point—I made myself
apologize, admit my grief's
been hard on people who aren't me.

Sheryl, sometimes I get sick of nuance
and complexity, trying to be fair
when that's not how I feel. I'm grateful
your book gave me the chance
to roll my eyes, scribble mean remarks
on sticky notes I hope the library
left in. I know that's not what you
intended, but like I learned from you,
when Option A gets taken off the table,
it's best if we embrace a second choice.

MY IMAGINARY THERAPIST

agrees when I say people suck.
She thinks it's unfair my dishes
still need washed, that I'm supposed
to care about my hair and where
I park. She's not surprised I find it
hard to sleep, leave my house
or hold my head upright. Like me,
she hates days with too much sun,
living so close to the beach
even snow can smell like salt.

She used to believe in lots of things
she doesn't anymore: God,
granola bars, the innate goodness
of the world, that consolation
is a useful goal. She doesn't offer
drugs or platitudes, guides to grief
that I won't read. She wants me
to eat more bread, pasta, potatoes,
all the ice cream I can stand.

My imaginary therapist agrees
cheese is the perfect food,
that it's a miracle I haven't killed
anyone yet. She's impressed
by my fortitude, how every week
I roll my trash bins to the curb,
then back again. She understands
I'm angry at the mail, friends
who ignore my calls or give advice
I hate. She believes I've earned
a medal, a parade, my name
engraved in bronze because despite
the pain I'm in, I still pay my bills
and usually don't litter.

Once, my imaginary therapist
confessed she wasn't sure
that she was helping, which only
made me like her more. We agree
it's stupid to have weekend plans,
wear pants without elastic
waists or pretend I don't crave
sympathy. When she calls me
her favorite patient, then says
she wishes that we'd never met,
I know exactly what she means.

Letter Started on My Steering Wheel

The mechanics I trust most wear flannel shirts that smell
of coffee and exhaust. They notice my low mileage,

how clean my engine is, say they can tell I've taken care.
When they offer me options for repair, I try to channel

your advice, then spend what it takes to ward off worry.
A week after you died, I went to get my car inspected,

was told I wouldn't pass until I drove two hundred miles.
The atlas in my trunk's a decade out of date, its pages

much too big for this new state, and yet I can't imagine
throwing it away. When I confessed that I was moving east,

you asked if I'd start talking like the people on *The Yard*,
and I said I'd do my best not to. I sound the most Missouri

when I'm tired or in pain—and also if a *y'all* or *fixin' to*
will get me what I want. A lot of what you taught me I've lost

by not using it—the names of trees and tools and how to win
at five-card stud, the best phase of the moon to plant

potatoes in—yet sometimes I'm surprised by my certainty:
From the sidewalk I could tell my neighbor's generator

needed new spark plugs, but didn't have the words for how
I knew. On the wall beside my desk, a shadow in the paint

suggests three-quarters of a skull. It reminds me of your
gearshift knob and hitch protector, the plastic skeletons

you hung in the back window of your truck. The morning
of the day you died, between Mom's calls I searched tickets

to Kansas City, sat staring at that skull. By the time
she said *Come now*, I felt like I'd been traveling for hours.

I won't call you my compass—it's not your fault how often
I get lost. You're my almanac and AM station, concrete

foundation like the ones you built so many of. You always
said you didn't fly because it was unnatural, but I know

you didn't like to ride with anyone you hadn't taught to steer.

BACK-TO-SCHOOL LETTER

In June, I heard the birds in the catalpa tree
call *Teacher, teacher,* then dreamed
I was late to a class I got lost finding,
where students from across my whole career
expected me to teach math and philosophy.
By mid-July I'd typed the dates for all
my syllabi, printed drafts I shoved
into a pile. It was too hard to imagine
past midterm, the day that marks
the first year since your death.

Faculty Welcome Day went better
than I'd feared. I think it helped
that I'd had dates for coffee one-on-one,
practiced saying how my summer was
so it seemed boring but not sad. A lot of things
on campus aren't the same: The trees
around Lot D are gone because of a disease.
Gaige Hall has that new-building smell
that probably causes cancer, but you'd love
the smart boards and student lounges,
view of the Union from the upper floor.
Because Craig-Lee is being gutted,
I moved to an office in the nursing school.
When I went to get my key,
I walked past glass-walled rooms
with rows of metal beds, mannequins
whose chests I checked for breath.

The room I spend the most time in is labeled
Manufacturing. Before my largest class—
thirty freshmen in Intro to Lit—
I steal chairs from across the hall.
I started them with Woolf: *On or about
December 1910, human character changed.*

In creative writing, one student
brought in *Little Women*; another, Tupac.
When my computer wouldn't work,
a biologist with his name on his belt
tested the outlet with a microscope
he happened to be holding, then filed
a request so one day I'll have power.

When I pass out the syllabus, I always say
there's a mistake I'll fix in a few weeks,
and every term that turns out to be true.
I like to think I learned that line from you,
but I've said it so many times I can't
really remember. Despite how much
about this fall feels new, I know
I'm not really starting over. I'm able
to go on because you're coming, too.

THE OFFICES OF GRIEF

                    are mostly beige and gray. It's rumored
there used to be plants—hardy ferns and philodendrons,

a ficus in the lobby—but after the last cactus died all traces
were removed. It's understood most people cry on their commutes,

need time to linger in their cars before they shuffle to their desks,
red-eyed but determined to be diligent. Recently a pod machine

replaced the Mr. Coffee that caught fire when it boiled dry.
Because mugs crack so easily, most folks stick with Styrofoam

despite its bitter taste. Each time the HVAC fails, the tech arrives
in cheerful coveralls, whistles while he unloads tools, but the hours

he spends banging in the basement leave him smudged and sad.
At first the broken elevator felt like a real loss. Then everyone

discovered stairs take less small talk, allow more time to choose
a floor. Besides, there's something soothing about cinder blocks,

the sense of being sheltered from great weight. To reduce insurance
costs, a nurse stops by two days a week. Mostly she treats

hypochondria and generalized fatigue, though she also offers tea
and pain relief, reminds people to breathe when their panic attacks.

Because the staff is overwhelmed by complex tasks, the managers
are never sure how much is getting done, but they've agreed it seems

unkind to ask. If an urgent order's left unfilled, invoices issued
in the wrong amounts, files found inside the break room fridge,

it's important to remember: As long as everyone's alive,
mistakes can still be fixed. Even the most devoted employees

don't plan to stay forever, but for now the Offices of Grief
give them what they most need: a place the stakes and lighting

both stay low and they don't have to hide how bad they feel.

BIRTHDAY LETTER

The morning I turned 38,
I pulled into the hospital before the sun
was up, mistook my phone's first ring
for something on the radio. Two floors
above, your Code Blue had just ended.
Doctors got your heart restarted
but you needed help to breathe,
and no one knew what shape your brain
was in. I didn't leave until long
after dark, until I'd signed a DNR,
cried in my car afraid to drive away.
E. spent the night with me but neither
of us slept. At 12:30 I saw the clock
and thought a call might come,
thought maybe you'd been holding on
until my birthday passed.

When I say I feel 85, I'm not
exaggerating much. I'll turn 39
on my busiest day: I might cry
while I drive to work, sit stunned
in my office before class, but then
I'll be with students for six hours
straight, get home too tired to do
anything but eat, fall into bed
already listing Friday's chores.
My birthday wouldn't be the same
without you anyway. Now it's also
the day your death began although
it took another week before doctors
were sure you wouldn't wake.
Your first death-day falls on
a Thursday, too, and again I'm glad
how many hours work will fill.

I don't think my grief will feel
this deep forever—maybe
next year I won't need to write,
will be content to just remember.
But I won't know until the days
I'm bracing for are over: the one
that means I've gotten older,
the one that means you never will.

Dear Atul Gawande,

When doctors asked who in my family
had a medical background, I didn't brag
to them—the way I sometimes did
my friends—that I spoke fluent hospital,
but I also couldn't stop myself
from showing off a little: Once, I held
my husband's gastro tube to free
his nurse's hands for something else,
once helped prepare a sterile field
around his bandaged leg. Once, I saw
someone shine a flashlight in his eyes
and asked if his pupils were equal
and reactive, once used the phrase
lizard brain to make a doctor flinch.

To show I understood the truth—
and to make myself feel tougher
than I was—I sometimes resorted
to the crudest terms I knew.
When his left pupil blew, it meant
he'd probably *stroked out*. If he really
was a *vegetable*, I was prepared to *pull
the plug*. I wouldn't discuss aftercare
because he was *leaving in a box*.
Yet I also said *yes* too often
that last week. In my heart I knew
my husband wasn't going to wake up,
but it made sense that without proof
we had to act as if he would—and so
the feeding tube, chest port for dialysis
that didn't work, the night I told
my resident the torture had to end,
morning I apologized for blaming him.

Atul, if I asked you to review
my husband's case, the narrative
I've lived with for a year, it wouldn't be
because I want to sue, blame myself
more than I already do. I'll probably
always struggle with uncertainty,
wonder what went wrong and why
I didn't know. But even if you couldn't
answer everything, I trust you'd
help me get my questions right,
tell me which skills I should improve
so I don't fail my next test, too.

Neighborhood News

Eight years after adopting my first dog,
I'm no longer shocked when strangers
interrupt our walks to tell me
how their own dogs died: cancer,
cars, poison, falls down stairs, old age
or fights with other dogs. I always say
I'm sorry, then try to get away,
but if they bend to pet my dog's gray face
or let him lick their hands, I may not
escape before they add, *I'll never have
another one, it hurts too much.
It feels like when your family dies.*

After my husband's death, I walked
the dog compulsively, grateful
to move my body through the world,
grateful this small need was one
that I could meet. Indoors, I watched
for signs that could mean canine grief—
excessive hunger, whining or fatigue,
needing to be retrained—knowing
no matter how he acted we felt the same
lack, longing for our old routines.

So far, I haven't stopped a single person
on the street to describe how my husband
died. But because I've been tempted,
I understand those dog-death stories
in a different way. They used to feel
like threats: *I lost what I loved
and you will, too.* Now I think it must be
a relief to have someone—especially a stranger
you won't see again—witness the grief
that no one else still treats like news.

LETTER STARTED JUST BEFORE YOU'D BEEN DEAD ONE FULL YEAR, THEN FINISHED LATER

All week I'd considered staying home
but wasn't sure how I could fill the hours.
Online, the suggested memorials involved
balloons and open flame, a kind of New Age
hopefulness I'm not willing to fake.
It rained so hard I barely dried my hair,
chose pants with hems that wouldn't drag.
At work I heard two women mopping
near the door: *She needs to understand it's all
just temporary. Ain't nothin' guaranteed.*

I'd thought once your death-day passed
I'd be able to relax, but the weekend
felt so slow I kept wishing it were over.
Monday the power failed at 2 a.m.
I hadn't known the storm was coming
but it must've been forecast: The neighbor
parked where there aren't any trees. I stayed
in bed an extra hour, dozed on the couch
because it was too dark to do anything else,
then piled fallen limbs along the fence.

At first it felt like a snow day without
the cold, concern about the roads,
but as afternoon began to fade I grew
desperate for noise. I didn't have a battery
for my clock radio, knew not to drain
my phone. Outside the sky held on to light
whose source I couldn't see, but indoors
I ate dinner in the dark, told myself
that my anxiety—like living without
power—would have to end eventually.
When it did I reset all the clocks and tried
to trust service would stay restored.

I've been warned that widowhood is harder
in the second year because the dead
don't feel as close. I haven't stopped
collecting news I think you need to know:
The actress you liked most walked off
your favorite show. Behind the bakery,
I watched a hawk hoist a live rat
into the air. Benny's is closing all
its stores, which makes me sad although
we never went. After the first snow,
I felt a draft and found most of the windows
were open at the top and must've been
since we moved in. I'm sure you'd say
it's not my fault, point out how far above
my head the windows end, how I don't raise
the blinds because I don't like direct light.

Before you died, I needed to believe
you heard me say I'd be okay, that it would
hurt but I'd figure it out—even then
I felt compelled to tell you the whole truth.
Although some days are uglier than others,
I think I've kept my promise pretty well.
When I'm tired of talking to myself,
I write so I can feel you listening.

Acknowledgments

Grateful acknowledgment is made to the publications in which the following poems first appeared (sometimes in slightly different form):

Alaska Quarterly Review: "Dear Sheryl Sandberg,"
American Literary Review: "The angry widows"
Birmingham Poetry Review: "Letter I May Never Finish"
bosque (the magazine): "Grief Logic," "Letter Started on My Steering Wheel," "Narrative Medicine," "Teaching Hospital," and "User Agreement"
The Chattahoochee Review: "The Offices of Grief"
descant: "My imaginary therapist"
Faultline Journal of Arts and Letters: "Grudges: A Partial List"
Meridian: "Interment Letter"
Natural Bridge: "Neighborhood News"
New Letters: "On days I don't think I'll die of grief,"
North American Review: "My dead husband"
Poet Lore: "Death Is Not an Emergency" and "What are days for?"
Salt Hill: "Letter from the Smallest State"
The South Carolina Review: "Preparing to Leave the Hospital: A Beginner's Guide"
The Southern Review: "Dear Joan Didion,"
Tar River Poetry: "Grief Land"
Zone 3: "Dear Mark Doty,"

Thank you, always, to Andrea Scarpino, who agreed that grief is weird and never wanted me to feel alone, and to Hilda Raz, who knew I'd write this book but pretended that she didn't.

Thank you to all the friends who sustained me: Kelly Grey Carlisle, emily m. danforth, Erica Edsell, Pat Emile, Lisa Marie Ferjo, Kathy Fagan

Grandinetti, Katie Kalish, Sandy Neumann, and Sarah Wilcox Elliot.

Thank you to the Keepers at The Bark Republic, especially Jess and Mike, who tended Sandbag when I couldn't.

And thank you to my parents: my dad for inventing the little man who lived in his shirt pocket, and my mom for letting the little man live with me after Dad died.

I'm also grateful to the wonderful staff at the University of New Mexico Press for making such a beautiful book, and to Rhode Island College and the members of the English Department for their support.

Bibliography

Alexander, Elizabeth. *The Light of the World: A Memoir*. New York: Grand Central Publishing, 2015.

Alexie, Sherman. *You Don't Have to Say You Love Me: A Memoir*. New York: Little, Brown and Co., 2017.

Bonanno, George. *The Other Side of Sadness: What the New Science of Bereavement Tells Us About Life After Loss*. New York: Basic Books, 2009.

Braestrup, Kate. *Here If You Need Me: A True Story*. New York: Little, Brown and Co., 2007.

Danticat, Edwidge. *The Art of Death: Writing the Final Story*. Minneapolis: Graywolf Press, 2017.

Didion, Joan. *The Year of Magical Thinking*. New York: Knopf, 2005.

———. *Blue Nights*. New York: Knopf, 2011.

Doty, Mark. *Heaven's Coast: A Memoir*. New York: HarperCollins Publishers, 1996.

Gawande, Atul. *Complications: A Surgeon's Notes on an Imperfect Science*. New York: Metropolitan Books, 2002.

———. *Being Mortal: Medicine and What Matters in the End*. New York: Metropolitan Books/Henry Holt and Company, 2014.

Gilbert, Sandra M. *Death's Door: Modern Dying and the Ways We Grieve*. New York: Norton, 2006.

———. *Wrongful Death: A Medical Tragedy*. New York: Norton, 1995.

Godwin, Gail. *Evenings at Five*. New York: Ballantine Books, 2003.

Hall, Donald. *The Best Day the Worst Day: Life with Jane Kenyon*. Boston: Houghton Mifflin Co., 2005.

———. *Without: Poems*. Boston: Houghton Mifflin Co., 1998.

Konigsberg, Ruth Davis. *The Truth About Grief: The Myth of Its Five Stages and the New Science of Loss*. New York: Simon & Schuster, 2011.

Maynard, Joyce. *The Best of Us: A Memoir*. New York: Bloomsbury USA, 2017.

Oates, Joyce Carol. *A Book of American Martyrs: A Novel*. New York: Ecco Press, 2017.

———. *A Widow's Story: A Memoir*. New York: Ecco Press, 2011.

Sandberg, Sheryl, and Adam Grant. *Option B: Facing Adversity, Building Resilience, and Finding Joy*. New York: Knopf, 2017.